OF GREAT IMPORTANCE

OF GREAT IMPORTANCE. Copyright © 2018 by Nachoem M. Wijnberg and David Colmer. This work carries a Creative Commons BY-NC-SA 4.0 International license, which means that you are free to copy and redistribute the material in any medium or format, and you may also remix, transform and build upon the material, as long as you clearly attribute the work to the authors (but not in a way that suggests the authors or punctum books endorses you and your work), you do not use this work for commercial gain in any form whatsoever, and that for any remixing and transformation, you distribute your rebuild under the same license. http://creativecommons.org/licenses/by-nc-sa/4.0/

Van groot belang © 2015 by Nachoem M. Wijnberg
Originally published by Uitgeverij Atlas Contact, Amsterdam

The translated poems "Another one to do again, about cultural Zionism," "Evening," "Into politics," "Like a law or a poem, for the Salafists or Constitutional Originalists, and are we now suddenly allowed to make jokes about what you're afraid of?," and "Nothing, nothing, nothing" were previously published by Poetry International Web (2017).

First published in 2018 by punctum books, Earth, Milky Way.
https://punctumbooks.com

ISBN-13: 978-1-947447-48-6 (print)
ISBN-13: 978-1-947447-49-3 (ePDF)

LCCN: 2018931072
Library of Congress Cataloging Data is available from the Library of Congress

Book design: Vincent W.J. van Gerven Oei

This book was published with the support of
the Dutch Foundation for Literature.

**Nederlands letterenfonds
dutch foundation
for literature**

Nachoem M. Wijnberg

OF GREAT IMPORTANCE

Translated by David Colmer

For in the soup or salad, or when you want to decide for others as if you can say, yes, you want to be king of Persia

The prisons cancel out the prisons

and wasn't it better under the Shah after all, the successor to Darius and Xerxes,

because if you discount drunkenness, was Khomeini so different from Alexander?

Do you remember how the last Shah wanted to build a new harbor,

where there was no harbor and no railway going there, and how were the construction materials going to get there,

and anyway, OK, a harbor, but is the sea even close to where you put your finger on the map?

You practice losing what you could say you had, like the pride and drunkenness of Darius, son of Hystaspes,

when he says yes, he does want to be king of Persia.

and later, as a reward, you can read the poem about it again, the book is lying open before you.

Themistocles says he can tell you, if you want to become king of Persia,

how to get each extra bit of land you also want to be king of,

and this time he really means it, it's not just a trick to get you to make a mistake.

The comparative method

Game theory doesn't help to find a solution, at most it's a way of seeing how problems can be compared to each other, that makes it part of the comparative method.

You read a history of something in which each event is compared to an event from the history of something else.

For instance, a history of the Ottoman Empire alongside one of the Aztecs.

Without one predicting the other, like the earlier testament predicting the latter, when the only son has become a Christian.

An old Jew sits on the ground gently weeping.

God says he can't stand it anymore, what's so terrible?

My son, the only one I have, has become a Christian.

Is that all? Just do what I did in exactly the same situation, I went to my lawyer and got him to change my testament.

That's what game theory was invented for, not what tragedy was invented for, and that's been invented at least three times.

The first time when a choir on the stage sings a text that doesn't mention the god of the evening.

The second time when an actor speaks to the choir wearing a mask that is so beautiful someone falls in love when they see it lying on the ground.

The third time when the listeners start to cry and are not sure why and the next day ask for the play to be banned.

Afterwards Aeschylus writes *The Persians* and Pericles pays for it to be performed because our enemies are big enough to stand on our stage.

The managers of the world

The demons of the past are negotiating about you
with the demons of the future,
writes Yehuda Amichai,
while waiting for one of the buses
whose routes are numbered with years.

What other demons
do you know about?

James Clerk Maxwell's,
who only allows the fastest ones through
to where it is cooler.

The Walrasian auctioneer demon,
who finds the equilibrium price
and announces it.

The Keynesian demon, slumped in his armchair,
who receives reports about you
every day,
but doesn't have time to read them all
or prefers a thirty-minute break.

He has already thought that the most terrible thing that can happen to you
can be caused
by things that are neither exciting nor deep,
and if it can be undone
it would be by them too.

Do you see a demon of the future
here anywhere? That must be the one
who tries to foist off as much work
as possible
(he's good at that,
apparently,

he could lead a large state).

Years ago he spent a week in a small forest
and he leaves it to the forest
to remember him.

Model

You bury your career in the ground like a flat model of the world with seas and rivers of mercury.

A career as a model, you know what that is, don't you?

In mathematics a model is something that fulfills a set of axioms, for instance a geometric object that requires all of these axioms to hold true at the same time.

A model like that can also be sent as a message.

For an economist a model is a simplified representation of a part of reality.

That economic model often includes a number of mathematical equations and they in turn require a number of axioms.

What is the question your model does not allow you to ask?

Now think about the state as a model and the highest laws as the axioms that model fulfils.

Can you imagine a state with only the axiom that if this or that is not unjust, then nothing is unjust?

That means that you must always be able to enter that state if you are fleeing from being treated unjustly in that way.

Otherwise imagine a state that enables you to no longer have to think: if I do that now I won't need to do it later when it might be difficult.

You have had a beautiful career, but now you would like to stay on for another week, a month, and if it goes well, maybe longer.

Because it is now evening, after a very sunny day, you dare to say that.

You only come back home later, knocking on the door as if you've forgotten the key but don't want to wake anyone.

Late at night, a model of the careers you have abandoned, but there are still a few left.

    envoi
Three rowboats
on the river,
secured to the bank
with an iron chain
and a small lock.

A bicycle thief
could open a lock like that in no time
and escape in one of the boats.

Selling

A boy wanted to learn
how to sell perfumes
before having to leave here again.

What do you need to know
to do that, sell perfumes,
not make them?

You start with recognizing smells
so that in the middle of the city,
you can say, there's the sea.

The boy came here
in a small ship to learn
how to be a seller of perfume.

Say you're waiting for a victory, somewhere, before you ask the price, and the reply will be, thanks for the news about you, now I am up to date

You listen to the news while doing something else because you could hear something that allows you to make a decision, but you don't, but the possibility that you could makes up at least partly for listening and what you are doing besides listening might make up for some of the rest.

Today you would like to be discovered as a professional investor and your discoverer can have half of what you earn from it, yesterday it was only a quarter.

How many times a day do you want to hear the news and how much of it would you like to be different from hour to hour?

Professional investors should not need to listen to the news to hear what they don't yet know, except when they think that that news will make other investors who hear it bid differently or that other professional investors will think so.

Do you not want to pay for the news today because you are afraid that tomorrow the price will go up?

Or worse, that you will be asked is that all, don't you want anything else?

Or worse still, you don't need to pay extra if you want more, and you haven't even paid anything yet.

They don't want you to think later, when you're old, if only I still had that money that I had when I could pay for things I didn't altogether want.

The most easily understood way of making a profit is selling something for more than you paid for it, for example buying something in a shop and reselling it on the street.

There is a possibility to do this if understanding or explaining something requires reasoning that seems difficult or painful, not because it is complicated, but because it clashes with what you would like to see as self-evident.

You can also wait for a panic you cannot fully share and then buy what others want to sell.

You do have to be able to bear losing at first because a good panic lasts a while.

Selling when you think that others are too keen to buy seems much more difficult to you because you are quick to think that others are too keen to buy and you would rather trust in a panic you don't fully understand or in any case haven't seen a reason for.

You speak as if there is always someone who listens when you want to say something and it's been like that for a long time, you must give investment advice.

Do you want to listen to the news now or not? You really don't need to make anything at all your profession.

At the market they dance carefully and slowly, as if they are no longer allowed to let the music help them.

Are you listening? You can also raise your hand if you are only half listening.

If you are already saddened or feeling pain anyway you can turn it into pity because there is always someone with the same sadness or pain, but you don't have to always become a professional at everything right away.

You have once again heard news that allows you to feel the way you wanted to and be proud of the one you pity, do you want to tell everyone else now and will they let you for a while, it's not often you get this?

You move your hands and fingers as if you want to sell everything you have left at any price, before the end of the market day.

A market day has a beginning and an end, which means that there is always a day's last buyer, like the last soldier to fall in a war or the last speaker of a language.

You should be proud of always hearing things last.

Is it easier to feel sad after being proud of something very small, like being the last buyer of a market day, but then not being able to see anything you really wanted?

The border

How many can you think about
at once? Say you get a job
that requires you to think about
one more. Like when you were asked
to decide where the border should be
between two states that were still one
at the time.

You know something else like that? The border
between the land of the dead on one side
and another land on the other side
or the border between day and night. And you don't
need to be king for a day to later be
king for a night in the land
across the border.

Would it help if you had an assistant
who could keep track of the extra one
for you, like the assistant
you saw in half when you want to demonstrate something
that nobody who isn't actually there
can believe? As a joke you ask
if she doesn't mind hearing,
off with her head. No, she says, as long
as you put her head on first.

Once you've done it once
you can start drawing borders everywhere
for better states than the ones we have now,
and you get a boy or a girl to help you,
but you alone must decide,
and the new borders will be announced
on an unexpected day.

Because you can't
please everyone
but continue to make decisions,
you receive as payment
calming beauty,
which is also something that you, when it happens more often,
find easier
to accept.

Today's classification problems

Today's three classification problems are:

classifying results or subjects of decisions,

classifying situations in which you can make decisions the results or subjects of which can be classified differently in different situations,

classifying decisions that differ in how much importance you place on how you feel as a person who has made a particular decision in this or that way.

If you can put two in the same category you can compare them and that makes it easier to choose between them,

but to weigh up two subjects or results of decisions against each other you have to keep them both in mind at the same time

or at least remember one while thinking about the other,

and then, along with the boundaries between the categories, you can also be worried about

the degree to which you are keeping both in mind at the same time.

What can you do about it? Ask someone else to decide with you

or let the most beautiful person you know decide for you, because they are so beautiful that a part of their beauty is

how little time they need to choose

between two chairs, two shirts, two of anything at all, and immediately afterwards no one wants to know why they have chosen the one they have chosen.

You wished there were elections today

and all the voters were beautiful in that way,

or would you rather postpone those elections a little,

just as today you want to wait as long as possible before listening to music that calms you?

The beauty that can cause a kingdom to fall

is so beautiful,

so much at the same time

that you can never be sure of your decisions as long as that beauty is in front of you.

Could you explain again what you are trying to do or want to do, for instance, what can you say about Iraq?

Sunni, Shia are their categories,
and that is another reason to ask a poet
(as if you've already asked
everyone else)
how to win the war in Iraq.

Nestorians,
are there any of them left there? You write them all
with a capital letter
because they are that kind of category
(like asking if everyone can be quiet for a moment
because you want to say something
that requires silence).

To say something about Iraq or something like Iraq
you need categories,
although if a category has a history
(which more people know about
than just you)
you can't say where it starts and ends,
just as you can't say that about a word you have just used.

But maybe you can
imagine different or new categories
so you can choose between them or within them.

Can you do it faster,
without all that ceremony,
faster than the shadow of a shadow for a shadow?

Wouldn't you have something better to say
if the one you longed for
asked you to say something?

Like the poet you heard about,
who kept reciting
because the representative of his desires
wanted something to write.
He asked, *why so many words?* but still kept going.

This was the poet who more than once
had someone who was with him
who he longed for more than the rest of the world,
but the first one never asked him
to say something.

He and nobody else had time to write something down
as long as the first one was still there.

Could you move the boundary between the category containing someone,
the umpteenth person to have long forgotten you,
and the category next to it, where you are,
an inch closer to you
to make more room for that person
so they don't need
to go away?

Could you do that for them?
Yes, if you could do it a hundred times.
Can you say that?
Yes, you can.

Something important
that changes the world
only happens if there is a lever
with a fulcrum you cannot
know enough about.

You are easy to silence,
letting you watch and guess if a lever is at work
is enough.

If you can make a boundary between two categories
shorter and shorter,
without distancing the categories from each other,
perhaps it becomes
a fulcrum for a lever,
not just a barrier.

Do you think you will be asked back
to say something more about Iraq
or will you try to long for Iraq first?

Don't forget, a state has a history,
which you are not the only one to know about,
just like a nation
(and of the two is the one that has the most history
locked in the prison of the other?).

Do you not want to rewrite the history,
even though it is the most important thing
anyone could ask you to do?

When you see the face
of the representative of the realm of forgetting
you are already long awaited
where you want to flee to,
that is Samarra, which is in Iraq, or Isfahan, which is in Persia.

If you want to wait for an answer anyway, wait for the blue sky to give you one, and remember a poem by Czesław Miłosz

When you wake up
you look at the battlefield in front of you
and walk around
to look at potential battlefields
not far from here
and roads you can flee on
and only then do you continue your journey.

Your supply of strategies
grows with every battle,
and you always try
to carry out so many at once
that you always
see a couple
go wrong.

A general who is good
at retreating,
that is no small compliment.

That is as if they
say of you: philhellene
and philo-Semite,
that can be the same,
a single coin with your head
neither on the front
nor on the back.

Because human reason,
beautiful and invincible,
makes no distinction between a Jew and a Greek.

Deciding what is a public good is also a public good, but every evil dictator can boast about the other public goods he has on offer — please, have another, no need to worry, there are plenty

Having to decide about everything yourself is unbearable — which in turn leads to the added value of having others decide for you, and the more power the one who decides has, the less you want to notice it.
If a poor, hungry man decides out loud for you, he's allowed to eat what you leave on your plate afterwards.
If the state does it in secret you are even willing to pay tax for it.
Considered like this, not only are the grass and the trees in the park public goods, but also your not needing to decide whether a stroll in the park this evening is worth two fifty, that is the comedy of the commons.
If a rich man can get a pauper to decide for him, he has less need of the state, and if every pauper has a pauper of their own the state can wither away completely.
Charles Dickens suspected that you would enjoy your hot dinner in your warm room even more if you could see a pauper pacing back and forth in the cold outside; this is his Christmas conjecture.
After half an hour you invite the pauper to come and eat with you and they get to say what the next course will be.
That way the pauper helps you not once, but twice — the Christmas and your birthday on the same day
conjecture — because you are also helped by the pauper deciding for you.
That is difficult — but not impossible — to explain to twelve-year-olds who do not want to surrender the two or three decisions they are allowed to make for themselves, no matter how sick they make them feel.

envoi
When Cleisthenes introduced democracy to Athens he made ten new tribes and each tribe consisted of three parts, one from the city, one from the coast and one from the interior, and each part was made up of ten peoples.

Your people were those who lived in the same area as you or where your family had once lived, if the other members of that people could remember.

Each tribe was given the name of a hero who was then considered the ancestor of all members of that tribe.

In the meetings in the Agora every citizen voted, but sometimes a representative of each tribe voted, for instance about which play was best.

Suggestion: take the map of Europe and make new tribes that each consist of three smaller parts from three European territories that are as different as possible, and so on.

Do you feel suddenly pierced by the arrows of time and how long before you will feel it again?

Just a little bit more about the way the conditions for allowing a market to function properly and those for allowing a democracy to function properly resemble each other.

None of the participants are allowed to decide how it will turn out next time; they mustn't even be able to predict it well; what happens next time must only be determined in part by what has happened this time.

The equilibrium price clears the market, everyone can go home, the fair price ensures that everyone goes home as wealthy as intended, and in a planned economy this is achieved with shadow prices, which in turn are derived from the costs of not being able to do something else.

It seems like a good idea to you to practice distinguishing them: the costs of regret, disappointment and disillusion.

That doesn't require anyone else and if you practice long enough there comes a time when you can begin to guess from which direction one of the three is approaching long before you can see which one it is.

The next time in a democracy is the next election, but how long does it take from this time to the next in a market?

It definitely hasn't taken long enough if next time the sellers are not able to lower the price enough for the buyers to no longer want to wait for the price to go down even further.

You sometimes try to imagine what a market would look like if you were sitting on the back of a moving price.

Economics might be the science that cries out most for thought experiments, but you almost never do them, or at least not openly.

envoi 1

Five percent interest on money you lend, as long as inflation doesn't rise too quickly or a war get too close, and ten percent profit on what you sell on — those are the percentages that belong to the length of a life.
But wouldn't they need to be changed, reduced, because lives have grown longer?
But it's only about the lives of those who lend money or sell things on, and they may have grown longer, but less than average.
But maybe those who are lending money or selling things on find the present more important than what comes later.

But do you know what the interest is now or will they only tell you if you really want to borrow money from them?
Or do you only want to know the price of something at the moment of the day when you can buy it or sell it?

envoi 2

How can what you feel be happiness? Just when it has become clear
to you that the plan you have worked on for years
will be a complete failure.

What you were planning is what you see has failed,
failures everywhere, were you really
planning that much?

Nothing, nothing, nothing

If asked why your café is called the Austerlitz Café,
you say there was an Austerlitz Café in the town your wife comes from and you gave your café the same name.

And then they say, I saw a Marengo Café not far away and a Wagram Café across the road,
and you say, they are owned by good friends, I have never asked them why they gave their cafés those names.

Then they ask if Napoleon was ever here or did he have something else to do with this place,
and you say you don't know much about Napoleon, but he was from France, wasn't he, not from here, and he conquered half the world, but not here.

Finally they ask if you are from here yourself,
and you say, no, from a small town up the road, but that town is so small, it's on hardly any maps.

Then you ask in return: would you like to do Napoleon, we still have the props and costumes from the last time we did him, you're free to take them,
but maybe you'd rather start with the revolution.

Who will do Danton, who will do Robespierre, who once saw someone buy something and it seemed so difficult he couldn't bear to watch,
and who will do Napoleon who comes in later?

You, you're always the proudest, you do Louis the Last and every day you write nothing, nothing, nothing in your journal,
or: liberty, liberty, liberty, or: nothing, liberty, nothing.

Your wife comes in and asks, did you go hunting this morning and did you shoot liberty?
If you didn't blow it to bits I can prepare it for dinner.

envoi
In your mind they are all ladies,
Madame Liberty, Madame Revolution, Madame Enlightenment,

and even if they're a head smaller than you,
they walk down the street as if you
can still see them miles away.

You can see me, can't you, why aren't you saying anything
to me?

And the way you walk down the street? With so many
coats on top of each other
your shadow fills the street
you are walking
through.

One day

In your career you haven't gotten further than the second lowest rank when heaven asks you for a proposal, and it doesn't even need to be yours.

What seems necessary is not just any proposal, but research proposals; a general model that helps say what you don't know enough about and then research proposals that help to find out more about it while also being partial solutions you can try out.

You can't imagine finding better proposals than those of John Maynard Keynes, who also had a general model, and you know how often he was mistaken anyway.

You remember his proposal that, if anxiety about the future meant that too much was being saved, you were better off spending the money you had borrowed from heaven on bridges and tunnels and escalators than storing it in the cellars of banks that will only dare lend it out to heaven or an equally reliable debtor.

You are exactly in the middle, below you the animals, with below them the dead animals, and above you the many ranks of angels with above them bluish gray heaven, who has angels to fill his glass and carry it behind him.

Every morning the angels come to the garden to be there when heaven looks around for the first time that day, but if his gaze rests on one of them, that doesn't mean they can hope for a higher rank.

One day you write a letter to someone else who is only something for a day, asking him to send you some of the gold that is lying around all over the place where he is, like dust on tables and chairs in a house nobody lives in during winter.

You haven't received anything yet and he can't have sent it on a ship that sank at sea because there is no sea between you.

He has so much of it he could bury part of it somewhere out of sight of everyone — that is one of Keynes's proposals.

One day he can announce it and then there will be work for everyone who can dig.

When Keynes is no longer there, Lydia Lokopova, Baroness Keynes, a former ballet dancer, feels the cold, because it isn't easy to heat the high-ceilinged rooms in the large house.

The wind blows through the walls, but she is not yet sure if she will have enough to spare this year to get them repaired — maybe she can hang paintings over the worst cracks.

Besides the Matisses and Cézannes (there are more apples hanging inside the house than on the trees in the garden), there are the paintings Keynes bought to help his painter friends or as speculation: in the hope that a day would come when he found them beautiful.

She has written so many checks, she no longer knows how much she wrote them for, but she does remember that wine from the cellar has to warm up and breathe first and puts the bottles in front of the fire hours before guests come.

She puts on a couple of old jumpers he used to wear when no guests were coming, one on top of the other, that makes her warm enough, and better here than in Russia, in the middle of the frozen steppe, beneath the clear heavens full of stars.

When the sun starts to shine again she quickly takes off all those clothes and runs into the garden naked — if anyone saw they would be most surprised, but why should it bother them?

You ask the other person who is only something for a day: do you have a wife? There are days when it feels good to be able to say my wife.

The abolition of debts

You become the first or last king because so much
has to be carried along behind you, your glass,
your beard.

They say all the land is yours
to give away,
but today you can also
sit in your garden and fill
your own glass.

But filling your glass
is also a rank at your court,
like that of the boy
who carries your glass behind you,
as if you and he are still the same.

Or rather, one day
during a thunderstorm
the king hides
and because they find you in your garden
they make you king for that day.

You sit on the throne
and they bring you food and drink
so that you don't need to stand up.

On the outskirts of the city
lightning strikes
where the king is hiding.

They bow to you
as a sign that you can stand up
and stay king.

The day that all debts
are abolished
must be an unexpected day.

Otherwise nobody
would lend anybody any more money
as that day approached.

Now that you are going to stay king
for longer than a day
you can say that
everyone who has debts
is free today.

Not the highest law, but the beginning

We start with who gets to vote

and what about and how many times

and who is stripped of their vote and for what reasons.

For instance, if a man is drunk on the day of the elections,

or his wife has died

and he refuses to bury her?

And where do the rules on this matter

fit into the pile of higher and higher laws?

What kind of exams would you make people sit

before letting them have a say on a proposal

like redistributing land?

Instead of making them sit an exam

you could remember that for a long time now you've been letting them make equally important decisions about you,

in that case they would be allowed to vote now too, wouldn't they?

Compare, if proposals are voted on at a meeting of representatives,

shouldn't people who can pay others to work for them, even if just for a day,

also be able to vote to select representatives?

envoi
You know how rare it is
to be made a citizen
in the city of ideas
and be allowed to vote
and get paid to go to the theatre.

Like a law or a poem, for the Salafists or Constitutional Originalists, and are we now suddenly allowed to make jokes about what you're afraid of?

How long can a text that is used to determine what to do remain as if nobody's?

A proposal: that can definitely no longer continue when a decision that required understanding the text has not been made for as long as a life lasts.

You have to decide: here is the text and what you know about those who wrote it, the previous readings of the text and what you know about those who offered them, and what you know about what they knew about those who wrote the text.

Is there anything else you want to know? The customs of those who live with the text and what they know of the law, and of its readings, and of those who wrote the text and those who offered the readings, and of you who must decide.

By the way: how long may a text that is used to determine what to do remain as if nobody's?

envoi

Let's make a law, then we can fine those who say something strange about it.
Or are we now suddenly allowed to say anything at all about a law, like about your nose?
Your nose is so long we know you are coming long before we hear your footsteps.
And if you stick your nose in your own affairs it sticks out the other side.
You have to pay as much as their face is worth if you bump into someone in the dark and you can still see it on their face a day later.

You are allowed to explain that law as you please, not like a joke that you are only allowed to explain in one single way, and the fattest angels and police officers keep watch.
Do you hear it still, and that too? Then you must have good ears, not just large ones, like your feet.
Imagine you couldn't kiss very well because your nose got in the way, and now you don't have a nose anymore.
Then you know a law you would like to start with.

One is already enough

As it's the anniversary of Hiroshima
(and by chance also your mother's birthday,
that makes it easy to remember)
you hope that the supermarket has a special offer
on something that removes cities from maps
(as if they had never been there, a mistake like Europe,
a traveler said he saw it in the distance
and a cartographer drew it on a map of the world
to make it easier to think about,
and later cartographers copied it),
because then you can also finally decide
when it is more or less permissible
to use it (if it is never allowed
you think that you might just as well stop
remembering wars).

You say, you need a nude model
because you want to write a history,
and preferably more than one, in case there's more than one
in that history, or more than one river,
and you remember a suggestion of yours
about how to defend a city far beyond its walls:
make the citizens train as soldiers,
(when they have a day off, but you don't want anyone
who doesn't have another job to take part)
and they stand their ground when you shout that the first attack is coming,
but run away at the second, now they have to get out of that habit,
and at the end of the day you arrive back home
and put on comfortable clothes to read old books,
on a warm evening, as it grows dark
and the boys and girls walk on the thick walls.

The community gives peace

If what is customary
is part of the law,
is that what is now customary
or what was customary
in the first community,
which was home to
the best decider you know?

To find out
what was then customary
you read what the historians
have written,
but what if they themselves admit
to writing speeches
to fit those who delivered them?

What would happen to the peace
if you arranged for those speeches
to be given in the theater now?

Do you, as if you
are the only remaining friend
of humanity, want to ban
all unimportant plays
and only allow those
that heighten the longing
for freedom?

Finding out
what is now customary
is even more difficult,
because you would need more than one life
to find out
what is customary
in the city you live in.

Unless there is
a market
for what is customary,
then you can see
what has changed price the least
because the most people
are offering and seeking it.

If you hear something for the first time,
you might not hear
how little it is,
like when you hear someone say that the community
gives peace.

You remember that you often
first hear sentences like that
in a dream.

If you hear a difference
between what you hear
and what you heard last time,
you can write a play about it
and have it staged.

You could wake up
in a theater,
among the audience
or between the gods
standing on stage.

And the community
gives peace.

As you've heard that before
you wait for what follows.

After the end of the show
you get changed
and go out through the rear exit.

Standing on the other side of the street
is someone who looks like you.

Concerning the limits to freedom of speech, in particular in relation to blasphemy, and the limits to property rights, *with hints how to be a good manservant, by a butler, written down to exercise his handwriting*

Suppose someone's wife has died, are you allowed to stand in front of his house at night screaming her name for a whole week? Or you scream fire, but it's not even busy on the street, it's late at night and there's no danger, unless people start thinking you know more than them.
You are not allowed to enter the houses of people you don't know at night and they're allowed to scream at you if they're scared because they see you standing there.
Are you then allowed to enter what they've thought about themselves, can that not also be their property, like when they've thought up some music?
But if the property rights argument applied, you should be able to say where the boundary is between what other people have thought about themselves and what you have thought about yourself, in which they, the others, may also occur.
What's more, the state can also place limits on property to serve other purposes, like insulting your master, if you think you are a servant despite that not being necessary.
To insult is to dishonor, but if you dishonor God and don't want to take the honor you have stripped away for yourself, you seek out someone you can give it to who is already so honored it can't do any harm, just as Wittgenstein wanted to give away everything he had to family members as they were already rich anyway.
There is a kind of property that gives you a right to refuse entry to those who could be victims and another kind that gives you a right against the state or God or nature.
God, you are not allowed to walk over my land unless you pay me, not even if you want to bury someone at night and you have to cross my land to get to a good spot.
Now a specification, not an exception, regarding the acceptability of insulting somebody's God (although do you actually know a God who's not anybody's?): if that somebody and their family are much less powerful than you, it is better to insult them in such a

way that they do not feel compelled to defend themselves to avoid feeling even more powerless.

What's more, if you insult the God of somebody who has much less power than you and they ask you if you wanted to insult that God or only meant that what you had heard about their God was not consistent with the dignity a God like that could have, it is best you seize that opportunity, which is a rare one, and say you meant the latter.

You want to make a genuine exception for someone who thinks they are the last servant of he who will never have another, that they are the last believer in their God; whoever insults their God definitely deserves death.

Don't forget that one of the charges against Socrates was that he didn't have enough respect for the gods, another that he made up at least a couple of new gods every day.

Let us then quickly consider the immortality of the soul, the servant of emptiness, the lover of memory, who when presented with an easy problem sees the solution immediately.

> *envoi 1*

Why shouldn't we blame Socrates for the fact that,
when the thirty tyrants, who were the fathers and uncles
of the beautiful youths he wanted to teach to think better,
as if a lion were chasing them
(it is only one lion and they are so many),
seized power, those very sons and nephews
prosecuted those who spoke against them
and called for their deaths,
explaining that they couldn't run the risk
of remaining calm and waiting?

So says Anytus, son of Anthemion,
one of the prosecutors, who in other cases
asked for mercy and forgiveness.

> *envoi 2*

Deep in the house of people like you who are really rich is the room in which you keep valuables and when you open the door such a glow comes out of it that you wonder if there could be a better place in heaven.

The things you buy and sell here constantly change in value, but if you buy a piece of heaven its value stays the same forever. Counted in what? In units of how you think about selling it off again.

Suppose heaven, hell and purgatory are exactly what you think they are, and when you start to think differently about them they immediately change to that too.

Or imagine, as Swedenborg suggested, that heaven, hell and purgatory are all here, in this world — you can't tell who's dead, but you must get a suspicion if you're somewhere and don't see anyone you dare to ask how they make their living.

Augustine said of a friend who later also became a bishop that he was determined to keep his eyes shut when he was taken to the arena by other future bishops, but once he saw the blood he couldn't take his eyes off it.

That was in the days when you could walk into a church and suddenly be made a bishop by the others who were there.

What can you do about it? Say that you're a tourist and a Jew to boot who is so sure of the non-existence of God that he can't imagine how he could be unjust to him?

That wouldn't help if they assume that the will of the multitude, in the church as in the arena or the theater, is the will of God.

As you are so rich, you organize a show in the arena and give away enormous cash prizes, not to the poor but to the hunters of wild animals in small enclosed spaces.

Giving away everything you have is not easy, for instance, first you want to give your neighbors or family members a chance to buy the things they don't want to become the property of strangers.

Do you think you should then also give away what you need to be able to spend the rest of the day together with someone without interruption, even with a pauper?

Or do you think that heaven is the country for the poor when the rich no longer need to die, which cannot be taken from them without paying at least double its value, but if there are no more poor people is it alright for you to walk around for a while in their heaven before turning off the lights and locking up?

Are you not then coming close to Voltaire's *I prefer my footman to believe in God because then he's less likely to pinch the silverware?*

For *footman who polishes my silverware* read *man I do not wish to do business with because he is too poor.*

If a poor man wants to give something to God there is no need to treat him differently, but if you hear that a rich man wants to give something to God you can't trust him as much as before.

You can do business with him, but only if he pays in advance and you can feel love for him if you don't want anything in return, as Spinoza proposes.

    envoi 3
Snobs mind us off religion
nowadays, if they can.
Fuck them. I wish you God.

So writes Les Murray
in a fantastic poem
about the death of his father.

Czesław Miłosz writes that, even if there is no God,
you mustn't make others sad
by saying so.

Yes, if those others imagine a powerless God,
you agree with Miłosz,
otherwise not.

Yes, if it's a God
whose compassion hangs him back up on a cross
(and he knows what it's like,
because he was just hanging there)
every time there's pain or sorrow somewhere.

After practically going to sleep with quandariness
about whom to give whom as a present,
you give Wodehouse to Wittgenstein.

What can you pay even more tax on and in which ways can you pay tax or what else could you do instead of paying tax?

A politician comes up and says, but all taxes are also wealth taxes because they reduce your wealth.

If wealth is what you have and might be able to use to make a profit,

is levying a tax on it comparable to making a company pay tax on the market it is allowed to enter?

Is wealth then also how long you can wait before making a decision, or only what you own and can sell, at least when you have nothing else left?

If we have a capital gains tax here, that means tax is levied on what you have gained this year, after deducting what has disappeared or been broken, but for that you or somebody else needs to have first written down what there was at the start of the year and provide proof of what really no longer exists — just thinking about how much there is to write down makes you uneasy — and that's why those who are able to write don't need to pay the tax.

Another tax proposal: the wealthy pay tax on the difference between the wealthy and the poor in their state and then the wealthy also have to pay someone who can write down for them how much the poor still have that year.

Here's a piece of paper to show the tax collectors, then they'll leave you in peace.

What's it say? What you've learned.

Can you hold back for a while on having to give lessons in that instead of paying tax?

What else can you do instead of paying tax and what kind of question is that for you, something like what do you prove by those who do not know you still wanting to see you?

Listening to music you can't distinguish from sounds you hear when walking the streets at night as a neighborhood watchman?

Who ask you if they are allowed to go inside or pull you inside.

In that case aren't the taxes you pay like someone else's for entering a market?

Imagine an exception regarding when you have to pay less tax no longer applying when your intentions do not coincide with the intentions the lawgiver thought those who would use the rule would have.

After all, you're good at recognizing intentions because you have had so many yourself: *I had them once too, a year ago.*

For example, the state says what a fair price for something is with the intention of allowing the sellers of that something to obtain a fairer proportion of the national wealth and you are already so wealthy and start selling it too, because you have so much of it.

What if the intentions of the present lawgiver are no longer the same as when the law was written, does that invalidate it?

What if the meanings of the words in the law or the intentions are no longer the same?

That also applies to poems and, if they're good, they stay valid longer than other texts.

(A poem being the most perfected of all texts is a misunderstanding, it is actually the one that calls out most to be improved.)

Is that why you propose that from now on laws should only be written as poems, and those who write poems like that should no longer have to pay tax?

Wasn't your proposal that the laws should be written down so that everyone can read them?

If there are people who are not yet able to do that, a teacher will be asked to teach them how to read.

But what can we do if they can already read but many of the words in the laws are no longer used and their exact meaning has been lost?

Or if those who still know what they mean won't say, like poets who only pass the explanations of words in old poems nobody else can read down from father to son?

If they use knowledge only they still have to write new and easier poems, it counts as capital and you can make them pay tax on it.

Taxes

A Muslim says, a Jew explained to me that religion is a form of tax collection.

The Jews paid tax to the temple, the Jewish Christians (who kept their eyes on the temple as long as possible every day because they didn't want to miss it if it suddenly collapsed) gave Paul permission to speak to non-Jews as if the temple had already collapsed, as long as he also made them pay tax to the community of believers in Jerusalem.

In the early days of Islam praying three times a day (later, more often) and paying tax was enough to make you a member of the community of believers and then you also got to share in the tax revenue; those who wanted to remain outside the community paid a different and higher tax and didn't share in the proceeds.

According to the Jew, this was a development of the Pharisees' idea that every Jew is like a priest and therefore has a right to a share of the tax paid to the temple, even if the Romans had burnt the temple.

Constantine gave a tax exemption to the Christian churches and priests, Julian the Apostate withdrew it.

Julian reopened the temples for the gods and also wanted to have the temple in Jerusalem rebuilt, but that failed because it kept catching fire, perhaps deliberately lit — that wouldn't have had anything to do with taxes, would it?

During the Festival of the Supreme Being, Robespierre used the Torch of Truth to set fire to a papier-mâché statue of Atheism and after the remnants had been swept up, a smaller statue of Truth was standing in the middle, black from the smoke.

Wanting to see how hundreds of cows and sheep were sacrificed, Julian visited the temple of Apollo, but only found an elderly priest trying to slaughter the skinny goose he himself had brought with him.

Do you think the Jews would have resumed paying tax to the temple if Julian had lived longer?

You don't think that particularly likely, unless the Roman state had assisted in the collection of that tax and that seems implausible, unless that new Temple Judaism became the state religion of Rome, in which case most Christians would have probably become Temple Jews and only a few of the remaining Jews would have become real Jews, like that Jew.

A Jew doesn't even think that obeying the law earns you a place in another world.

No other people is so attached to this world, because they don't think there is another, except maybe tomorrow's, and when they hear it starts today they don't hurry.

You hold a mountain over the head of a Jew and tell him you will drop it if he doesn't accept the law you want to give him, what do you think the Jew will say?

He accepts it, but will remember that it wasn't of his own free will, so he can leave it behind somewhere later and not walk back for it if others yell after him that he's forgotten something.

The Muslim says that the other Jews bribed Paul so that he would propose that Jesus was God instead of just a prophet.

Anyway, how can you recognize a prophet if the Jews are not against him?

A Jew saw Muhammad and another Jew asked, are you sure he is the prophet who has announced our law?

The Jew said yes and the other Jew asked, what do you think of him?

By God, I will be his enemy all the days of my life.

Lawgiving

Can you think up a law
about someone who has something happen to them
when it happens to someone else?

If you have decided
that a law you have thought up
is valid you can write it down,
so that it can be broken or torn down the middle
when saying goodbye
and each of the two can take half,
as if they wouldn't recognize each other
unless they can show
the other half.

You can also write the law down
where nobody can read it all,
but you have one person read one part
and another another part,
and so on,
and they in turn can divide up
what they have received.

You can also call a notary
to write down
who gets to read
which part
if there isn't enough time left
to give it to others
to read.

So much for this one
and so much for that one,
you are dividing it up again,
and if you need help with that
you choose the cheapest.

Think of the law as land,
not yours perhaps,
because you're not a man of the land, are you?

But imagine,
a friend you no longer expected
comes to visit you,
why would you not call a notary?

And why
would you not say yes
if that friend says
that rather than putting him in your will,
you should put in a state
that will immediately sell what it gets from you
to be able to buy more land?

Because that state doesn't have nearly enough land
for everyone who might still want to live there.

What a luxury,
you have a long day to think up a law,
but you still can't decide
that one is valid,
because it doesn't lead to different outcomes
that you cannot imagine
simultaneously?

You're no philosopher king, after all,
standing in a high place like King Saul,
dropping something and walking away
because it takes too long
to hit the ground.

If this or that law applied,
who would you never be able to see again,
or only just before the end?

Remember, the most brilliant laws
are the same for everyone.

Making someone king

They come and ask
you one by one
if you could maybe
make someone their king.

Then one of them
who thinks he has something
to pay you with
comes up.

After you have made
him king he goes back
to working the fields
as if nothing has changed.

They come back again
to ask if you will again
make someone their king,
maybe the same man.

Have you taken something
away from one of them?
If they think so, you want
to give it back right now.

Speech, speech

You have learned a speech by heart
in case you go through the wrong door by mistake
and end up on stage,
in front of a full theater, the powers-that-be in the front row,
and if you didn't have a speech they might think you wanted
to carry out a coup.

It is the speech
a boy wrote for you
for the wedding
of a bride and groom neither you nor the boy had ever seen
before,
and after many other speeches.

Remember the times
you saw actors who thought something was happening to them
but it wasn't.

Oh no, you can't remember that
because you don't like
sitting in a theater.

If you can still remember
that you too have power,
one play after the other is staged in your head,
that is one of the reasons you find it difficult
being part of an audience in the theater.

You are the first to have his speeches written,
by the boy who had dazzling loves,
one after another.

Going back home

The inventors of coins
minted coins with their heads on them
to pay the Greek soldiers
who come from such a poor country
that they want to serve in armies far away.

The other soldiers can be paid differently,
but if the Greeks go home
they need to be able to pay with something
and sell what they don't
take with them.

Markets are hurriedly opened
just outside the walls of small cities,
one after the other,
as you approach,
on the way back to Greece.

Back in the city you come from
you can have a coin reminted
with the head of whoever you want
to be exiled
and vote with that coin.

If you are exiled you get all the coins
with your head on them, you can live off them
for years.

Into politics

If you've worked for someone else who told you
how they wanted to be with you, are you still allowed
to go into politics? You are here.

You can pay someone to do your work for you
if you have enough to pay them and then you can
go into politics, at last.

You don't pay tax anymore, but as if representing
the state in your purchases you buy a
warship or a play.

What else can you do instead of paying
tax? Say that those who have less than you
can come and stand before you
and tell you what they want
to tell you?

Or do you not mean those who have less, but those
who are so ugly you are not calmed when you see
them voting?

The long wave

Gangsters like Lenin or Mao don't allow you to just keep quiet, you also have to say that you agree with them, over and over, more than once a lifetime, they increase a freedom only to punish you and everyone else who makes use of that freedom — that's a strategy to make it more difficult to remove them from power. Compare, why and when it is a good idea to switch between nationalizing and privatizing an important industry such as banking or the railways.
If each of the two has advantages and disadvantages, the disadvantages generally increase the longer one of the two continues unchanged, but switching too often has disadvantages as well, and that's why you propose that most citizens in a state should only experience an industry that was nationalized being privatized again or vice versa once in their lifetime.
The older your citizens get, the more time you want to let pass. When things went wrong with Lehman Brothers you quickly proposed nationalizing a few banks in the Netherlands and were called a Marxist, although surely it is the opposite of Marx to want to save capitalism in Europe at the beginning of fall, at least as long as you stay living here.
Now your state wants to sell a bank it bought to stop it going bankrupt, but why shouldn't it keep it for a lifetime?
There are enough non-state-owned banks left to ensure that competition in the market for banking services will not be disrupted and even if the state-owned bank were to be less efficient because it is state owned, that doesn't seem to be a problem, if it doesn't function as well it will become smaller. The state could make that bank behave the way it would like a bank to behave and if it turned out that this made it difficult to provide certain banking services, the bank could stop offering those.
This way the state could immediately establish experimentally which banking services can be better provided by non-state-owned banks and a new law could be written about what banks are allowed to do simultaneously, so that a bank that wants to provide those services cannot provide others together with them,

like savings accounts, which make it difficult for the state to allow that bank to go bankrupt.

Make a bank, or something else, larger and smaller a number of times, and perhaps you will better see what the law about it can be.

Smaller if close enough to bankruptcy that you have to run and save it, larger if close enough to not having enough space and needing part of the future.

Do you need to add that one of your grandfathers banked with the Amsterdamsche Bank, later the AMRO, later the ABN AMRO, whereas your other grandfather banked with the Philips Bank, later Mees, later ABN AMRO MeesPierson, and that Philips Bank belonged to the Philipses of Zaltbommel who received a visit from their nephew Karl Marx, whom they paid an allowance as an advance on his inheritance from his mother, who no longer gave him anything herself?

Now to explain once again why codes of conduct and other forms of self-regulation are weapons of the social-corporate-responsibility accomplices of the gangsters' corporations?

Or swear an oath again to follow a code of conduct, or is it already too late and would you prefer to go home now?

Power brings responsibility because if poets had more power, you would hope that you too would get to be responsible for something?

The power of corporations far exceeds that of individuals, but the state does not allow individuals who want to drive around drunk to set their own rules.

Why should Shell or KPMG or the ABN AMRO be given more freedom to make decisions about how to behave when those decisions can cause greater damage than a confused or clear-headed person who can get drunk or think they can bring the world to come closer?

envoi 1

Suppose it was all intentional, the state buys big banks when they are in danger of bankruptcy and sells them again when the economy has recovered and they are worth much more.

That way the state could nationalize and privatize almost without having to decide to do it.

In this way the market would do for the state what the state does for citizens when it makes decisions about things the citizens no longer want to or are no longer able to think about because it is too difficult or takes too long.

And suppose it was all intentional, and to get Greece and Portugal and Spain to leave the Eurozone, the European Central Bank offers to cancel the debts those states or their banks have with that bank.

To do that the bank increases the money supply, which reduces the value of the euro and makes interest rates rise.

That way the economies of the remaining euro states do not contract while the prices go down and the European Central Bank stops exports from declining because the euro is too strong, just as it would have also needed to do if the Eurozone hadn't broken up.

The remaining debts in euros are also less difficult to repay for the countries that have left the Eurozone and they can carry on with economies that have grown more strongly than they would have without the euro.

The greatest advantages are for those states that retain the euro whose governments have quickly borrowed as much as possible at the low or even negative interest rates available before the break-up of the Eurozone so they can spend more.

After the break-up those states can pay back their debts at low interest and in cheaper euros — that would be so clever if it were intentional.

If you who are reading this no longer need to die, allow me to remind you that Greece was a weak state with a weak economy and both were further weakened by the influx of borrowed money enabled by Greece joining the Eurozone, and when the banking crisis broke out at the start of the twenty-first century, Greece had a public debt that was impossible to repay.

envoi 2
Shall we go somewhere
where we can speak
about why today the banks have run out of money
and the states have run out of money.

On the street in a city
where we have never been together before
or in a restaurant at the station,
waiting for the train back.

Borrowing from the Greeks

As if you are Ptolemy Euergetes,
you ask the Athenians
to lend you Aeschylus, Sophocles and Euripides
(the manuscripts of all their plays,
including those that are later lost)
and you give them fifteen silver talents
they can keep
if you don't return them undamaged.

You copy the manuscripts
and return the copies,
not secretly, but as if standing on the stage,
immediately explaining that the Athenians
can keep the fifteen talents
as a fine for what you've done to them.

Further questions about the relationship between specialization and temporary employment contracts

Half a lifetime ago it was less strange to apply for a job you didn't have the expected education for, and if you had a job it was also not so strange to be asked to do something other than what you had been hired for — if they gave you time to prepare yourself, it should be possible, how difficult could it be?

Specialists are getting better and better at things regarding which a non-specialist is unable to decide how good they are at them, and that makes it more difficult to do something you haven't done before.

You also get less and less time to learn to do something better, because otherwise you will have already left again before you peak — doesn't that make the price for rare specialties go up while the price for the less rare goes down?

Something else, what is the smallest unit of time you can imagine writing, like a lawyer who says, I had a brief telephone conversation with a client, put ten minutes on the bill?

Does being good at more than one thing at once make it easier for specialists to write smaller units of time and would that not also make it more reasonable to give them shorter temporary contracts?

Increasing specialization also increases the need for accounting rules that incorporate evaluation decisions because how else can someone who is not a specialist decide how good a job the specialists have done?

This in turn increases the chance that decision maker too will become a narrower specialization because how could someone without the appropriate professional training know how to deal with the decision-filled accounting rules?

If the accounting rules allow an undesirable decision to be made, when do you choose to change the accounting rules rather than setting this decision apart from others that have been made according to the rules?

Imagine your decision maker is your representative to whoever or whatever does not need to die and the only one who can do that for you.

Imagine whoever or whatever does not need to die can arrange your day so that you find it easier to wait for something you cannot do anything about.

If you then want to keep increasing your decision maker's pay, will you no longer want to do that when your decision maker doesn't need to die anymore either?

Because you want a remuneration rule to be derived from the gratitude you might feel.

But what does that mean for the relationship between a remuneration rule and a compensation rule, like when you've injured someone so badly that they will not be able to work in their profession for a year and you have to compensate them for their expected income in that year?

If they earn ten times as much as you, you have to pay it to them, if necessary by borrowing money at an interest rate that depends on how long you will live and how long you expect to keep your job.

If you injure someone who has only had short and uncertain employment contracts for as long as they can remember, you can estimate their expected annual income as lower than the average for recent years, but what if you injure them for the rest of their life, which will last as long as they want it to?

If you make a decision about someone, short employment
contracts for the person you have to tell your decision to have
another advantage for you: if they are disappointed or angry
because of that decision they will be gone again soon.

    envoi
In the third large organization your father worked for
it occurred to him that all large organizations
were like that (in the first, he thought
he was unlucky, in the second,
that he was to blame).

For a day

First I am king and then you
and then me again, like when the Romans
name kings and fire them again,
and they can be as big a king as they can afford
by selling ranks at their court,
there are still plenty who would like a rank like that
if they already have everything else they ever wanted,
and they order magnificent clothing in which
to appear in the palace when you open or close the year or the week
or, if they're in a hurry, the day.

When I am king again I will make you
my advisor because I know that you have already spent a long time
thinking up advice you could give someone
who is the last of something, like the last king
of Assyria. Remember, each of them
decides alone, not as if he is one of two or three
who are just like him. I want to write what I still remember
of the last advice I thought up in the ground
around me with a stick like a spear.
Yes, and then I have to decide
before stepping out of it.

For the Romans, a philosopher king
is just a servant who can work for them
in two ways, like a plumber king
or a philosopher saxophonist. But the last time you
were king you said unnecessarily loudly — because even if
you whisper there is always someone to tell the Romans
what you have said — that you still wanted to learn something new,
begging if need be, or did you know something better
to learn? You've wanted to know for so long whether it is better
to start early in the morning or be the last one left

late at night. If someone can teach you more about that,
let them come to the palace immediately,
you will pay them by the hour,
you promise that and you say it out loud.

If it is my last day and yours
is long gone, I make the Romans heir
to everything I have ever had. You only know
someone's abilities and desires after
they have ruled. That is why it is good
for as many people as possible to have been king
for a day — or longer, if they are slower — and
why we are so grateful to the Romans
for firing kings and naming them the way you or I
order coffee in a café that has just opened
early in the morning. What a disaster it would be
if we were to one day hear that yesterday
was the last day of the Roman Empire.

    envoi
If you hoped for power you never got,
like the king for a day's,
it was only to give the most beautiful one what she wanted.

The only thing you have left now
is what you can remember when you choose,
the most beautiful one being with you, not because of what you
could give her, because you couldn't give her anything.

Not really rich

You think about what you would be like if you weren't rich,
but you're not really rich, not really poor either,
you don't have any houses of gold and marble,
but maybe a small house on the coast,
where you go when it's too hot in the city,
and you can drink wine
when you eat with your wife and friends in the evening,
which is in keeping with the best way to grow old.

You are rich enough to go for days
without having to do politics or business,
when you might be able to write something
your friends may call pompous,
because you know that what you write will not always be remembered
and then you would rather be pompous than ironic.

What are those days like? You wake up,
think about what you want to write,
walk into the garden and write more afterwards,
you eat something small, then stroll
to where you can look out over the sea,
back in your house you read a speech from a book
out loud to yourself, which might have once
been an exercise, but now you are no longer sure what it's for,
you sleep for half an hour and take a bath,
then eat dinner with your wife and maybe a friend,
then another walk after it's already dark.

Because you write histories
you think about those who are in the history
as if they are taking an exam with you.

You think up answers
they could have given,
like when you want
them to pass as quickly as possible
except the few who don't need your help.

You know more about what you have been given than you do about who you are talking to

You have been given a small part of a decision,
like a square meter of land,
along with the two or three people who hardly have room to stand on it
and pay their tax to you,
you also pay tax for them.

You hope to be paid compensation
when somebody else frees them.

You can honestly think that this is just,
because you have been given that decision or that square meter
and those two or three people.

Do you already know what is left if you subtract them from it,
not just how to add them to it,
like when you want to imitate someone?

The only reason you know
for wanting to free one of them yourself
is seeing him in a play
and his being just like you
when you are on the stage.

Thank you, and what are you, a historian in a hurry or a hesitant futurist? Or: I will do what you have hastily asked of me, but then I don't need to go to your funeral

An *Or-else-we-get-this* rule is what takes effect when something else does not take effect or appears when something else ceases or has not come about, and is also how something is understood if there is not a convincing reason to understand it differently, or if the convincing reason no longer applies.

Will you take into account that the *Or-else-we-get-this* someone else is using can take effect earlier than the one you are using when you both have to decide on what will, in retrospect, be a mutual decision?

But that would mean that France and Germany can force each other to make decisions that will leave them both worse off in the end.

Ah, thanks for reminding me that World War One never started.

How can you have been here so long and still understand so little?

Someone saw you here and didn't think it was going very well.

As if you are the one who has to decide if there is sufficient reason for something.

envoi
The *Or-else-we-get-this*
of a text is
that you have written it
if you do not know or are unsure
who wrote it.

Honor

Does honor make you want to flee
if someone with less power than you
acts like that is not the case?

Like seeing someone on the street walking towards you
who you could have freed
and they don't greet you.

That is what you say in the fat man costume
with an extra belly and extra thighs
and all kinds of add-ons
that make walking difficult,
as if you're more than one person.

Honor is what you are proud of,
like you are proud
of being able to do business with anyone.

That is the honor
that reduces the likelihood
of your having to leave here,
because then the others,
to whom you were so generous
and who have promised to help defend your honor,
would be sent away with you,
as if you were a state
or a street.

You stand in the street yelling *usura, usura*
because you want to do business
with those who have more honor than you.

Honor is like air,
something you like to get
without having to plan constantly for it.

The air
Falstaff talks about,
which the man who left here on Wednesday no longer inhales.

You can eat out for the rest of your life
thanks to that air.

That's why they only give it to those who are already faraway,
and here they only get
statues or streets.

Starting with
Mandelstam Street.

Do you still have enough honor
to walk down that street?

Representative

You do not need
to work for a factory,
you can also be a representative
with your own business,
you know what that is, don't you?

A suitcase in each hand
with samples
of what you can produce in your factories.

You make each profit four times:
when the customer orders,
when it's delivered,
when the customer pays,
when you get your commission.

You earn little,
then a lot,
but at the end of the year
you only need to worry about your factories and customers,
not about what your boss might think.

You have known your customers for so long,
they will be sure to pay.

It's not going well,
your customers say,
maybe it would be better
if you slowed down a little,
and on business trips
only *ate* in grand hotels,
sleeping somewhere else.

On the stock exchange

If those who don't need to die invest on the stock exchange
they are losing every day,
because in the best instance someone like you sees
the approach of what is close by,
whereas they only see
the approach of what is still faraway,
that's why they are such bad investors.

It is difficult for them to wait and do nothing,
they buy and sell every day.

Neither do they have any friends
who can lend them money
if they have lost so much
they cannot continue
that day.

If asked for advice
about what to invest in, ask in reply how long the person who is asking
expects to live.

You are not allowed to trade in something yourself
if your decisions, other than as an investor,
have an effect on the price,
or if you have been asked for advice
by someone whose decisions have that effect,
or if you taught them about it
long ago.

But if you have received news in a way that is permitted to you,
you are allowed to give the impression
that it was the opposite of what it was,
by selling when you want to buy
and secretly having it bought back

by someone they have never seen
at the stock exchange.

Do you feel uncomfortable about
knowing so much,
do you want me to stop telling you about it?

You know so much
and sometimes you are the first to arrive somewhere
— you look around and there's no one there,
would you like to leave and come back in again later? —
and it happens
that you are half told,
like when a hand is laid on your shoulder,
that the person walking towards you on the street
doesn't need to die
or all of those walking towards you on the street
in a small procession
and their music comes later, that's still faraway.

If you want to explain something you can start here

You keep shoes in which you can no longer
walk properly, that's against something,
isn't it?

You receive an invitation
and say that you will come on foot,
and then you look for a pair
of those shoes
and you have plenty to choose from,
because you have so many
of them.

Halfway you realize
that you have forgotten to take
what you wanted to show them
and that is why you make
something that doesn't even
show how hastily
it was made.

If you want to explain something about money
begin with: money is
for trading and saving,
and then ask,
as if you can put your hand up if you want to answer,
what else can you do that with,
both those things?

Putting up your hand
is like deciding whether to walk on
if what you have heard
is a price,
and hoping you'll have something left later,
when you no longer know what you can quickly make from what
you can see.

Ten, ten, ten

Genghis Khan divides up the Mongols,
and those who are sufficiently like them,
once again,
in tens,
hundreds, thousands, and tens of thousands
who are together
as if they all share an ancestor,
like the Athenians who were divided up again by Cleisthenes,
but not like ten Jews who have come together.

As he and his Mongols
do not read or write,
each order is made into a rhyming couplet
to be included in a song
the tens,
hundreds, thousands and tens of thousands
sing as they march.

You hear,
the Mongols are Jews,
but how can that be,
they don't know a thing about the law of the Jews
and what's more, can Jews even sing?

They are the Jews
who followed the others
until they lose sight of them
and now they think that they must first conquer the world
before they can decide about something else.

The Jews

Do not touch my Jews,
the king says.

Do not set fire
to their houses.

They accept your clothes
as a pledge.

And if you repay,
half is mine.

And if they are no longer here,
the other half too.

Do not touch my Jews,
the king says.

Otherwise I will let
my Jews loose.

What is the difference between his Jews
and a bank today?

Nobody dares lend their savings
to the Jews because the king will take that too.

How then do the Jews get money
to lend out?

They borrow it from other Jews who live in other kingdoms
and hope that they will flee in time with the money in their
suitcases.

Look, there's a Jew running
with a suitcase in each hand.

That Jewish

You recognize how happy
you would be to be an idolater,
you are still that Jewish.

You only stop making images
when you notice you're not getting any closer to what you see
and that it's your fault.

You are also a slow runner
and end up standing still
as if you have forgotten
what you were doing
because beauty was running in front of you.

You do all that
and still remain a Jew, even one
like in a picture of
how there is a Jew hidden
behind every barrier and impediment.

The Jew is the adversary's sidekick, the prosecutor,
and if they can't find you
they ask him: *say something about Jews,*
and when he's finished talking
he lays his hand on the place where you are now hidden.

If you long for something
you try to make what you find important
the counterparty in your transaction.

The Jews

The Jews have been given so much history
and in the little the Christians have
the best is over right at the start.

Christians don't have much geography either,
the only place they can point out on a map
is where Christ is for sale every day, and today
is a clearance sale, at least that's what the Jews say.

Do you know the joke about the Christian Zionist?
What is that? A Jew who asks a second Jew
to ask a third Jew for money so that a fourth Jew
can travel to Palestine. But how is that about
a Christian Zionist, it's about a Jew, isn't it?

Yes, but it is about a Jew who doesn't want to be like the Jews.
Yes, a Zionist, but how is it about a Christian?
Well, the best is over right at the start.

Why not like those Jews? Because they try
not to show what they fear or long for,
because they don't have anything
that can't be taken away from them at any moment.

What nonsense, it's not just from Jews,
everything anybody has can be taken
away from them at any moment.

Suppose you were not a Jew, but wanted to become one,
the other Jews advise you against it and tell you
you're better off staying Christian and asking for help
from the son of God who hid in the belly
of a Jewish woman for nine months and then came out
and let himself be taken prisoner. If you weren't told
a story like that as a child you would find
it difficult to take it seriously.

Feel free to ask them more questions,
for instance: if a son has become Christian,
is he allowed to say Kaddish every day of the year
of his father's death? Compare: if the father
has only become Christian to be better off,
not because he no longer wanted to be Jewish,
the son is allowed to say Kaddish
every day of the year of his father's death.

How can a Jew who is actually
no longer a Zionist make himself useful?
By acting like he is on a desert island
where a single Jew has been washed ashore – and yes, if he could,
he would have left long ago. He tells visitors
about the two synagogues:
one he doesn't go to and he can't remember
the last time he was in the other one.

Does Moses die at the end of the Sabbath
or at the beginning? If you haven't asked the question yourself
you can also say, let all of us together
— including the poor man — go to yet another
and ask him, like when they came to you with the question
about the poor man — they had brought
him too — and everything he did went wrong,
he and everyone else were long used to that, and now he had
asked a woman
to marry him and she had said yes.

It must have been at the beginning,
because on his last day
Moses writes all the books of Moses once again,
as if he doesn't know what to do,
but wants to have tried every possibility,
and if it was already the Sabbath he couldn't have done that.

Your friends come to visit and ask
for your help — that is their way of helping you —

because you are not yet used to having
so little power. You cannot do
what they are asking, but send them to someone else
who goes with them to someone else again
and finally they reach someone
who wants to end this.

There is theater that reminds the audience
of a community they could be part of
and there is theater that doesn't do that
and is called banished. If the Jews
want to make the first kind of theater
they have their actors exaggerate as much as possible,
because there are only three or four of them
and they have to fill the whole evening.

Another one to do again, about cultural Zionism

Going to Palestine to speak and write Hebrew and starting by translating in your head what you heard people say as a child walking on the street,
        and leaving their languages to the Germans and the French because they need them so badly, *und jeder soll nach seiner Façon selig werden.*

Or speaking Yiddish as if it's Arabic,
        also as a trick for when you bump into Arabs who are family, who have made such an effort to forget you and you have forgotten them.

Or you want to start by learning Yiddish because people who already speak and write German
        hardly need to do their best to understand Yiddish, that's an advantage of Yiddish over all other languages.

But for that very reason it's easy to lose something important when translating from German into Yiddish or vice versa,
        so maybe it would be better to speak French in Palestine.

You can easily mix Yiddish and German when speaking, or else you Germanize or Hebraicize your Yiddish, and so on, one language after the other,
        around the world in six days and on the seventh you are silent, nodding at another old man you see on the street — why are we all so old?

You want to rediscover the truest feature of your people there where they are the most left behind,
        and then search for what differs most from what the rest of your people have or what most resembles what those who have been left behind by other peoples have?

What they have forgotten to get rid of and then no longer dare to get rid of
>because it reminds them that they too once asked: but do you want to get rid of me?

If you want to make your writing as true as possible, do you try to make it sound old
>or the way someone writes who hasn't thought in advance about how to tell a story and just starts hacking letters into a rock with a chisel?

But the least changeable qualities will surely be the ones that are not lost when they are mixed with those of others,
>and they make it possible to scream Jew, Jew at someone who writes in German or French?

What can be said about all Jews, or at least about all the good ones, besides their not believing in God,
>or passing through history as the opposite of the Weltgeist that makes clay from shards and houses from clay?

If the Jew wants to have a state, why in Palestine, why not in Europe,
>it must be possible to found a state where you already are.

Which state is not also a prison of nations,
>a few more added every day?

You have always wanted to found a state in which you could change who you ask for help if you want to flee
>just as easily as you change your opinions — and you don't even need to flee.

Yesterday you thought that the Jews would no longer want to have a state if they all got much older,
>but today you have a different idea, so new that you don't need to apologize for the old one.

You read the declaration of independence as if you are an actor who wants to make the audience cry, if necessary because his acting is so bad,
> because he is not sure he can get them to laugh.

If you say that I am listening to you as if I have promised to die for the state, you are probably right,
> and then I would also say what might make me die for the state or the state for me.

In Zion the Jew would be too busy building houses and living in them,
> but in Europe it is as if he has been naked from the day of his birth and has never visited a barber, but this morning they dressed him, gave him a shave and cut his hair.

You can always continue longing for Zion like Yehuda Halevi because he thought he would have good neighbors in Jerusalem,
> if he had bought a house there the price would have gone up because of the neighbors or perhaps because of just one neighbor.

> *envoi*

What a surprise, Zion being like Sicily,

almonds and laurels.

My dear Jews,

shall we have breakfast first?

There are three possibilities,

but the one on the square is best.

They have tables on the sidewalk,

but if you go down the hall past the kitchen you come into a small courtyard.

Der Judenstaat

Compared to other nationalisms, atheistic Zionism is one of the most reasonable.
It would be even easier to call it reasonable if serious reparations were offered to the Palestinians, financed by a tax on the value of land that was a Palestinian's and which a Jew received too cheaply, and by a collection among the diaspora Jews who want somewhere to be able to flee to.
Like in the blue-and-white tin from the Jewish National Fund that was put on the table when other Jews you rarely saw came to visit, for instance on a day in a week of mourning — that money was used to buy land.
And now we're on the subject, how much for the rest of the world?
But if the land remains the problem, when, under which circumstances, can you start a state, is it necessary for that state to have its own territory?
Couldn't the Zionists have started without territory?
There are enough states with territory, but without private land ownership, so why not the other way round: private land ownership but a state without territory, except the land that is the property of its citizens?
But a state Jews can flee to if they no longer know what else to do, is that possible without that state having a territory you can point out on a map of the world?
That doesn't need to be a problem if the Jews can say: where I live now is in the Jewish state, even if I leave it when I go out onto the street, but I don't mind always carrying my passport with me.
Home is where the heart is, and the Jewish state can be where a Jew is, if the other states would be so kind as to recognize it.
The state the Palestinians now have comes close to being a state without territory, even if its recognition by other states is still incomplete — not only by Israel, it would be nice if a man who can say that he is a citizen of the Palestinian state was permitted to become a dentist in Lebanon.
For that reason too, it can be said that Zionism has made the Palestinians scarcely distinguishable from non-atheistic Zionists.

Before you forget, there must also be a simple way for Jews to indicate that they do not want to be citizens of the Jewish state, for instance by saying that they are just as happy to be proud of *eine Fahne zu haben, ein Kriegsschiff zu sein. ("das stolze Kriegsschiff...")* Your father described a mourning visit to the house of a man who had five sons: all five of them stood next to each other saying Kaddish — *I agreed with that man about almost nothing, but that looked tremendous.*

Now send someone or go on a condolence visit to someone whose five sons are all dead; you now live in his house, but you know where you can find him.

The promise

The only purpose of
the story about
the promise is you
having something to say in reply
if they say to you:
you are robbers,
because you are taking the land
of the Canaanites.

You do not want
to shame the one
who promised it to you
and cannot speak well
— who chooses Moses because
he is just as bad at it
and cannot even say
his own name.

Moses came
from the west,
the land of Egypt,
and traveled through the desert
for forty years,
emerging east
of the river.

He looked
to the west
when he was standing on Mount Nebo,
from where he could just
see Jerusalem
at the start of
a clear evening.

The Jews

The Jews have won again,
and are sitting on cane chairs
(left out on the street
because they are missing a leg)
on the veranda
in their own state,
not in one of the almost empires
of one of the great-grandchildren
of one of Alexander's generals.

They have a king
of their own again
and can tell him:
cut off your own head,
if he asks them
if there is something he can do
to increase the chance
of their feeling at ease about
him walking through their streets at night with his wife beside him.

Speak up

If ten
come together
they can begin
a Jewish people.

If ten are already here
the others can stay where they are,
who wants to be just in time
to be tenth?

You keep watching
to see the eleventh,
who is no longer trying hard
to be tenth.

What kind of deal
do these two make
if they can still both
be tenth?

They ask each other
to make peace,
the last one to do it
gets nothing.

Would you like
to be the umpteenth today,
like Abraham
the most righteous?

To whom it was said:
go from your country,
later you will hear
where you can stay.

A voice
in the wilderness:
make a path
for my people Israel.

Do you have
a people then,
aren't you just someone
standing there?

You just act
like you are
hiding behind
a tree, a hill.

So that no one
can see
where your voice
is coming from.

    envoi
Let he who brings peace
to the high places
give peace to us,
and all of Israel,
and say: yes.

A proposal for Happiness Day

A tax proposal: people and organizations negotiate which organizations those people are members of and to what degree, and those people then pay their taxes through these organizations, in proportions that correspond to their various degrees of membership.

Organizations can be corporations, but also families or sports clubs or political parties or maybe even the group of all those who would vote for a particular proposal if given a chance to do so.

It would be easier for the state to collect taxes if it only had to deal with organizations rather than individual people, and if the negotiations between the people and the organizations failed, a representative of the state could impose a reasonable outcome.

Then there's the problem of how to share power within the organizations, because in the Roman Empire taxes were imposed on organizations such as cities, and the rich and powerful of those cities got to decide how those taxes were to be shared among the inhabitants, how do you think that went?

This is part of a larger problem because the richer and more powerful people or organizations become, the easier it gets for them to pay less tax.

The rich and powerful can quickly hide their reserves by converting them into different reserves, even if they are slightly drunk, just enough to once again see something that is so beautiful they would rather piss their pants than take their eyes off it for a moment.

Remember how every state you know has developed towards a condition in which the rich and powerful do not need to pay any tax at all, like the nobility and the church in France before the Revolution.

Don't forget that a state that cannot collect enough tax from its own citizens and organizations is more likely to consider a proposal to invade another state to sell the citizens of that state back to themselves.

You thought you were only being asked to make a proposal, but now you're being told that it's your problem that they don't have enough of what it requires?

It cannot be the case that if there is an army too few where another army is waiting, you end up having to walk there as if you were an army?

If not enough taxes are collected here, we can have it done by tax collectors from faraway, but the revenue stays here, they only come to help.

The honor of the state forbids it? Is that the pride in the history of the state and everything and everyone the state wants to be heir to?

If you have to pay your taxes in something other than what you have, there needs to be a market where you can sell what you have to spare to get what you need to pay your taxes and there must be a road to that market.

Which you can also use to walk home with everything you had with you on the way there, if evening has come, and you walk unhurriedly because of the emptiness inside you which is not a bad thing.

Until game theory was invented it went like this: if you wanted to say something about a coming war you studied history, like a lawyer who wants to say if a case stands a chance.

Since its invention you start with a proposal about which decisions could make which future decisions impossible and which of them you will still be able to reverse later.

What a disappointment, a war has broken out, armies are crossing borders everywhere.

Who will now have time for your proposal, which cannot succeed if you cannot convince whoever you had in mind when making it to participate or at least let themselves be reminded of it?

Another tax proposal: we will retreat from a tax on profits to a tax on turnover in the market of the state and simultaneously allow export subsidies.

That could also help to make a minimum wage apply to the whole world, how could that be?

An organization that has goods made in a state that doesn't impose this minimum wage is not allowed to sell in the markets of states that do, except after payment of a market tax on top of import duties, if the latter still exists for those goods and between the state where they are made and those where they are to be sold.

The extra revenue from this tax could also be used to repay some of the costs of those who have not received that minimum wage and wish to become citizens of the state where what they have worked on is being sold.

Objection: if states tax entry to their market, won't the prices in the stores in those states rise and won't other states want to profit from this by not charging this tax and won't the rich be more liable to travel to shop or send someone else to do it for them, no longer doing their shopping in the states that have imposed the tax?

In that case a state that does charge this tax can impose high import duties on goods from states that do not, and maybe a small exit and entry tax as well, the level of which will depend on the wealth of the traveler who is departing that state for a non-charging state or returning from one.

Or else travelers would be obliged to spend a certain amount in the country they are returning to, again dependent on their wealth, within two weeks, just as you used to have to spend at least twenty-five marks a day when traveling from West to East Berlin.

You also propose to make it easier and more attractive to be a citizen of more than one state, just as it has long been possible to be a member of many organizations at the same time.

So easy that the average person would be a citizen of ten to twenty states and if you only had two or three passports everyone would laugh at you.

You could also become a citizen of each state you work in or pay tax to or lend money to by buying part of the national debt or by finding a citizen of that state who will let you call them mother of father, and call you son or daughter in return.

In addition the states will give civil rights to those they wish to honor — that is not a new proposal, the first French Republic already did just that, offering honorary citizenship to people faraway who were struggling against tyranny and superstition, from Joseph Priestley to Friedrich Schiller.

You pay your taxes to your different states in proportion to how much of a citizen of that state you want to be, which gives you a corresponding share of civil rights and a corresponding claim on public goods.

Again, just as in the first proposal, there needs to be a way to decide if you and a state cannot reach agreement — perhaps it would be best to have the United Nations General Assembly decide once a year, on Happiness Day.

And what if two states in which you hold citizenship get into a war with each other?

If you can, you decide which of the states is, according to you, more in the right than the other, and then lose your civil rights in the other state for the duration of the war.

If you can't decide you continue to pay taxes to both states and if you get drafted, you serve for so many weeks a year in the army of one state and so many weeks a year in the army of the other, again proportional to the amount of tax you pay each.

You get a letter of safe conduct to go from one state's army to the other, subject to a number of reasonable limitations, like not being allowed to change sides in the middle of a battle, even if you have completed all of the weeks for the army you are in.

You recognize this problem because you remember your Greek teacher at secondary school relating that during his medical for the draft he had honestly told them that he was a member of the Pacifist Socialist Party — which still existed at that time — though not really a pacifist and that was why he was keen to complete his military service in the Dutch army and learn how to handle weapons — but he wanted to honestly warn them in advance that the moment World War III broke out, he would try to desert to the other side to use what they had taught him in the Soviet army.

Sending the army of a state into another state is more likely to be a good decision if you can make a profit from it because then you will be more likely to be able to pay reparations later for any damages you have caused and cannot justify.

So, yes, it was more reasonable for the United States — because if you want to think about something like this you start with today's most powerful and most beautiful state — to send its army to Iraq rather than Zimbabwe.

A problem of the state in international law is that domestic territory is defined as being inside a state, and every square meter of ground is inside exactly one state — can you drop that assumption so that multiple overlapping states can be recognized?

That is why you propose being able to proclaim an almost state, like one that could now be given observer status at the United Nations.

That is a step in that direction, but further gradations of statehood could also be introduced so that a state would become more of a state as more people were prepared to participate in that state as citizens, reducing their participation in another state, as in the proposal that everyone can be a citizen of many states.

What's more, as long as states can have the greatest power over people, people should be able to start a new state if they have a reasonable concern that their rights could be reduced because they are seen as a member of an organization without necessarily having chosen that themselves and not being able to leave it easily *and* not being able to rely on another state to defend their rights with force or at least being able to flee to that state — you want to call that the Zionist principle.

This newly founded state is not allowed to use force to make all members of that organization its citizens and nonmembers must also be able to become citizens of that state, even if they make up the majority in the state.

Surely it's beautiful that so many non-Jews would like to live in a Jewish state, maybe even a reason to found another?

You can invert this too: a state that helps with the realization or continuation of such a state does not need to give asylum to those who want to enter it because their rights are being restricted in the state they come from because of their membership of such an organization.

This should also apply to the citizens of states that are so poorly led that their civil rights fall below a minimum, comparable to a minimum wage.

Those who cannot obtain minimum rights or a minimum wage must be able to obtain asylum and citizenship in another state, unless that other state is willing to help them set up their own state.

One day a certain Dr. Kafka came to visit and you advised him to look for a job in insurance.

You remember what it was like there or you continually see how different it is here, those are the two ways of being exiled.

You look startled when you recognize someone and only then do you remember what they are to you.

If the one helps you, the other, the opposite, does too, surely, like seeing and being seen, going to live in Persepolis or in Petrópolis, especially if you have to remind yourself of what can help you?

Did you also advise Dr. Kafka to become a Zionist, and if so what is the opposite of Zionism?

The glory of having not just one state, one language, one religion, but as many as we want.

Remember the lonely man Herzl, who nobody ever visited anymore, but they came in their thousands by train and on foot to his funeral at the *Zentralfriedhof*.

When he entered the theater the Jews whispered to each other: *here comes the king.*

They laughed at Herzl because he wanted to found a state with its own nobility and medals.

You don't need a king to distribute ranks and honors at court; you can do it without a king, and to you that seems appropriate for Jews.

You wanted to be able to be a citizen of more and more states, then you could feel calm and happy when they became increasingly shadowy.

After you have become king of the Jews, you have a play staged in such a way that not a single member of the paying audience can leave, and those who are at home and remember those members of the audience are ready to burst into tears.

But if they really don't want to listen anymore, you go out on the stage, rip your shirt open and say: here is my heart, and you cry.

There is more reason to limit the freedom of the theater than the freedom of the press, because in the theater they are already sitting there ready to think about nothing except the performance.

Is that the way it works here? If the revolution has come, someone goes on stage and says lines that are not part of their role or, if they are part of their role, now with a new meaning?

The problem with acting, its not being real, surely only applies if you are doing it yourself and don't have enough time?

There is also that other problem, that you are almost always so scared before going on stage that the one time you are not scared makes you feel uncomfortable.

When you are on stage to tell the audience something you hope that, if it doesn't go well, two other actors will come and stand to your left and right, with you in the empty place between them.

Compassion and recognizing injustice take up room and that is yet another excuse for not finding out more, because you don't have that much room.

But you can see a play about it and that gives you more room than you thought you had, just look at the stage, you could put dozens more statues there.

If people can participate in several states would you like to also allow states or other organizations to participate in another state as if they are people?

Preferably not, but you can imagine making an exception if it's a state in which almost no one wants to participate anymore, then that state could ask one of its last citizens to participate on that state's behalf in another state, or it could ask someone who is very poor and has few other means of making money besides being paid for something like that.

When states make treaties with each other in which they give organizations the right to defend their interests against the states' before a judge who will be easily convinced to take the organization's side, without giving their citizens equally strong rights against those organizations, it can be reasonable if those states are weak and led by less competent governments, but if that is not the case, these kind of treaties make it more likely that it will be one day.

Even on days when you are hoping for a future with weaker and weaker states you don't want the states to weaken while organizations grow more powerful and the members of those organizations have even less to say about decisions that can change their lives than the citizens of states.

Do you know a way to give people more rights, including against the state, without other organizations getting more as well, thus making the people worse off?

You could give people more rights against organizations first, but how could they enforce those rights without help from something like a state?

Maybe the states can become weaker, but can a citizen of many states collect so much power from so many states that that combined power can counterbalance the power of organizations?

Just quickly about rules that say: you are allowed to be this or that or do what doesn't harm others, but if it involves something you can change yourself, this right is limited by your having to do your best to make sure that those who find it uncomfortable to watch can escape it.

You cannot imagine any kind of state without such rules and that is why you cannot propose a universally valid objection if you are told that you are allowed to be Jewish, but not in ways that make it immediately visible to everyone on the street.

In turn you would like to propose two exceptions to that.

First, if not being allowed to show something increases or strengthens a lack of freedom.

Second, as long as people are allowed to want to flee to your state because they are not allowed, even secretly, to be this or that in their state, it seems reasonable for it to remain permitted in public in your state, if necessary in a designated place in the middle of the state.

What could also help is declaring a state legally incompetent, which is not the same thing as a legally incompetent government — if the state is legally incompetent no government at all, no matter how competent and powerful, can make binding agreements in the name of that state.

The debts a state makes while being governed by a legally incompetent government — or one that turns out in retrospect to have been legally incompetent, although we could not have guessed that when doing business with the state at that time — can later be declared invalid by a new government — after a revolution, for instance.

The state can apologize for what people have done in the name of that state, even for things that happened hundreds of years ago, just as you can apologize for what you did yesterday.

And people can offer their apologies for a state, why not?

Have you apologized for Cyrus and Darius, Xerxes and Artaxerxes yet today?

You might not be a citizen of their state, but you can't say you haven't benefited from it.

If you were only allowed to apologize for things that only you could have done something about, it would get sad so fast.

How quickly nobody would be able to stand it anymore.

Deciding

In the quietest world
even you can make a decision
after having thought about it
all the time.

From the moment
you are asked something
until you have stated
your decision.

If you are asked
to judge the intent,
you judge the results
and the other way round.

As if your only defense
is that you have seen
enough differences
today.

(It is evening
and you want to run to where
the rain intended
to fall.)

Back in the USSR, for Faiz Ahmed Faiz and Alessandra Palmigiano

A reader of Marx from Pakistan
visits a military cemetery in Leningrad,
when the Soviet Union still existed,
and writes about those who bought the future with their blood
and gave it to those they would never meet.

He also writes about Chopin,
and for a moment I think that Chopin belongs to me more than to him,
which immediately shows how little I know.

Tell me, comrade, how you, when evening has come
walk to your father's house
in the hills,
where your father no longer lives,
but where there is still someone to turn on a lamp when morning has come.

When your father had a house for after work,
on a mountainside,
not far from the small town where he was a doctor,
there were two palms in front of the house,
the trees standing upright in the sloping ground.

Your father ordered truckloads of soil,
which he spread with a metal rake and tamped down,
because he wanted flat ground
on which his children could play
and look out over the valley.

The two palm trees are still there,
the lower parts of their trunks hidden in the earth.

What is it like in a country
inhabited only by heroes,
who haven't been in their own home for a long time?

It is not good for a house
to stay empty for a long time.

The trees lose their leaves
and vagrants try to set fire to the dead wood
to keep warm at night.

Sigmund Freud visiting Constantine Cavafy, or vice versa, but they had told each other that wouldn't make any difference

Imagine you are
a blind old man
and nobody wants to come sit next to you
except your daughters
or your sons,
all in uniform,
because the war has begun.

All you know now
is that someone can have more than one life,
just as they used to have more than one soul,
so they could send one away
and not let it back in
until it had returned
from a long journey.

Do you think it is necessary
for you to know or understand more
than those you want to help?

You hoped that talking might help
and wanted to get them to talk about history,
but almost no one knows anything about it,
that was why you let them
talk about what it was like
when they were so young
they hardly remembered anything from all those days.

Didn't you find it difficult
to listen to?

When does history
change into
a memory
and you no longer know
when it is from?

Giving counsel

Xenophon asks Socrates for counsel about his plan to travel with the Greek soldiers in the army of Cyrus, who wants to become king of the Persians instead of his brother Artaxerxes.
Maybe he can later become their general if they want to return home, or he can try to become king of Persia himself if they want to stay there.
Someone or something will speak to Socrates if Socrates remains silent for a long time, either heaven, or a demon who acts like he is at home, or a god, like the god Apollo, who promised Achilles a long life.
Socrates says that doesn't happen often anymore, he never knows when in advance; and what's more, even if someone or something were to speak to him, he could not ask questions or pass on the questions of others; Xenophon would do better to seek counsel in Delphi, where Apollo answers.
Xenophon goes to Delphi and asks to which god he should make a sacrifice in order to ensure that his journey goes well and he returns safely.
When he comes back Socrates asks why Xenophon did not ask if the journey was a good plan, but now that he has asked something else, it is better for him to stick to the answer.
Something else, you know that Apollo can be bribed, and if you pay more than anyone else could pay, you can write your own answer.
But surely that alone is no reason to stop taking the answers you get seriously?
Or do you want to collect those answers and save them up, so you can use them when you are asked for counsel?
Then you, just like Themistocles, could be banished because everyone has had enough of you always being right and then you would have no choice but to accept the job the king of Persia offers you.

envoi
Suppose that, faraway, heaven
keeps adjusting its hypothesis
about how well you can predict what is yet to happen.

For so long, heaven acted
as if you could give it counsel,
but after so much time it no longer needs that hypothesis.

Suppose a boy or girl is told:
you have to try to become king of Persia,
and you once heard
that was possible
and have been reminded of it now.

The successors' strategies

In the wars between Alexander's generals the loser's soldiers join the victorious army, as the winner will probably be able to pay them sooner and better.

That is why a general does not choose the strategy with the best chance of winning the battle, but one that delays the soldiers' seeing that they are not going to win for as long as possible, by which time it is probably too late to start negotiating.

At the same time a general tries to make it as easy as possible for the opposing soldiers to join his army, by saying in advance which terms he is offering, and if there is no time left to negotiate, they only need to make a vague gesture to accept them.

The older the soldiers, the greater the chance of everything they have being transported in the train of the army: the general who captures the adversary's train does not need to offer the opposing soldiers much else afterwards.

The soldiers no longer know if they can return to the place where they were born, as their enemies might have come to power or it might now cost too much for them to live there, even if they sell everything they take back with them.

The more often soldiers desert from one general to another, the better they are at their trade, and meanwhile they have become old men who can remember many almost identical contracts, while still able to stand unmoved with a spear in their hands.

The final battles are still won by the last soldiers who can remember how they shouted at Alexander that if he wanted to conquer more of the world, he could do it on his own.

The besieger

Do you start by laying siege to small cities
or large ones?

If a siege fails and you have to withdraw,
other cities will not surrender
as quickly.

Do you hope that there is at least one person in the city
who has nothing to gain from things staying the way they are
and opens the gates for you?

If you want to allow someone else's soldiers
to join your army, do you hope that his army is as big
as possible?

But what if you have so few soldiers that they look at each other
in the afternoon and disappear when it
gets dark?

Do you build many small ships or a few
enormous ones?

A large ship will defeat a small one,
but do you dare send it out to sea
as readily?

And what then? Are you going to end up
hiding your large and mighty ship
underwater in a port?

They call you the besieger
because you besiege so many cities.

Do you take them too? Not often.

Demetrius Poliorcetes

After Demetrius, the great general,
gambler, drinker, rider, lover and economist
(not necessarily in that order, with an economist
you always need to add that),
conquers Athens for the second time
he asks all citizens to come to the theater
and when they are seated
he walks quietly down the steps
until he is standing on the stage
and when he is standing there and speaks
they can hear him well.

As a lover he is best of all,
because there is always a moment
in which he thinks that the one approaching him is a god,
a beloved husband and father,
an honest merchant,
a friend of the poor,
and he has never understood
what is wrong
with thinking that you are with more
than went out with you.

Plus, he is also praised
as a god
— in Athens they sing:
the other gods are far away
or do not exist.

Later he gets no more help
from Athens
and the Macedonians make it clear
that they would rather have Pyrrhus as their king
and when he tries once again

to conquer Asia
his last soldiers desert to Seleucus.

    envoi
You can compare Demetrius Poliorcetes with Demetrius
Phalereus, the philosopher of the school of Aristotle, who
governed Athens in the name of Cassander until Demetrius
Poliorcetes conquered the city for the first time and Demetrius
Phalereus fled to the court of Ptolemy Soter in Alexandria.
When Demetrius Phalereus governed Athens it had become too
expensive to perform entire tragedies, instead he had poems
recited in the theater.
In Alexandria Ptolemy built the great library and Demetrius
Phalereus
helped the librarians decide which version was best if a play or
poem was not the same in different manuscripts.
The painters and sculptors in Alexandria started making work
that was so realistic that, seeing it for the first time, birds and boys
acted like it was real.
The poets of Alexandria started writing poetry not just to listen
to, but also to read, and that is why they were able to make it more
difficult to understand immediately.
Plutarch compares Demetrius Poliorcetes with Mark Antony
because they both always chose large and many, even if they didn't
have a choice.

Speeches

You are citizens of one of the Alexandrias,
and once a year,
on an early summer evening,
the old men come and stand next to each other
to recite speeches
from four or five plays
(the speeches you still have,
you can only guess
the rest).

A traveler (who had arrived
that day) said that you
should send your row of old men
to one of the other Alexandrias
to take part in a competition
for choirs.

Another traveler (who did not come together
with the first) said that you
should not do that,
because what you listen to
does not make you feel what it is like
to go through difficult times
and does not give you the hope that it would therefore
be easier if you went through them
in real life.

In a store

You go into a store
and ask the salesclerk a price.

Can he show you something else
and something else again?

You hardly look
and forget almost immediately
whether what he was holding
a moment ago
was more or less expensive.

The owner is in the back
in an office with a bead curtain
instead of a door.

As long as there are no other customers
the owner cannot blame the salesclerk
for being patient with you.

How can you go into
another store later
without a small chance
of overwhelming and answered
longing?

Something else, quick,
so you can move on
with another memory?

Procession

You want to be the kind of sculptor
who has made so much money
he can go into politics.

Your studio full of statues,
and if you line them up one behind the other
they're like a procession.

You want to be the kind of sculptor
who can replace the head of one statue
with another.

You only notice it when,
like someone who's blind or in the dark,
you run your hand over the face
and throat
and feel the fracture.

In the middle of the night
you walk to your bedroom window
because you hear a procession
passing on the street
of those who are going to leave you on your own.

You know you have to say goodbye
to what is almost finished
saying goodbye to you,
the whole procession like a little boat
on a quiet sea.

Evening

Cavafy writes about a young man
who didn't yet know what kind of career he wanted,
but thought that he still had ten more years
of being handsome enough to be let in there, where he stood outside in front of the door
in the evening.

He was a customer there,
but thought that he would still be handsome enough for that
for ten more years.

Cavafy writes somewhere else that he is moved
by a detail in the coronation of John Cantacuzenus and Irene,
daughter of Andronikos Asan.

He can say that,
just as he says that it's almost evening.

If colored glass instead of gems
symbolizes what is appropriate to have
on the occasion of a coronation or a marriage
that is made perfect
by holding the lightest possible crowns above the heads of the bride and groom,
what is then appropriate to have?

State and market

If you are the highest representative
of the state
you walk across the market.

Where too little is being sold,
you buy what is left
before the wholesalers
make a low offer
when the day is almost over.

Or you offer loans
at an interest rate that is lower
than the banks are asking,
so the sellers can wait a day longer,
the state will earn money then too.

You start selling
what you have bought from them
when the prices have started rising
as if people are expecting
them to go up even further.

And if they themselves still have
what they can sell for those higher prices
you let them pay off their debts.

Remember, it's also your job
to keep fear and pity
apart.

Looking at the market as if looking at the stars and the state as if looking at the moon in autumn

You are standing on an empty stage
and have to explain what you see.

For instance: I am now standing in a corner
of a busy market.

Now you can be made a representative
of the state at this market.

The inspector who can tell if weights are true
by picking them up.

Because you have never been mistaken
about whose poem it was.

Judah Halevi

You believe with perfect belief
(the *quia absurdum* refers
to perfection)
that you are at the most distant point
of the west.

That is why
you want to travel east
across the sea
where it is stormy for a day
and then calm for a day.

A girl
who is like a gazelle
stands next to you on deck
(a gazelle would find
it frightening).

You said where
your heart was so many times,
you had to travel there.

Will the one who seeks you
find you in Jerusalem
writing in the sand with a stick?

While the city is once again
taken and destroyed.

Have you arrived there
where you can see that your lover was
the night before?

Nobody there recognizes you,
but when you see two boys looking at you
you walk over to them

and ask them
not to tell anybody you were here.

Today

Today would not be a good day for

the last conqueror of the world to arrive
and kill or enslave everyone,

but if there any poets, he would like to give them a small gift.

But you don't know if you

could stand in line today and say who you are,
and say thank you for what you get

and plead for the lives of this person or that person.

The luxury of not having to say so much,

being able to start with: when are you going to make a list
of everyone you want to invite to your coronation or wedding

and write addresses on envelopes?

Or are you putting that off, because the next day

you are going to follow them up with uninvitations
and go outside to invite

those you can still find on the street?

      envoi
After a day's hunting and fishing — without catching
anything — you can be a critic in the evening.
You wonder if there are enough things to review, but if we, for
instance, decided that cauliflowers were funny, each of us could
bring along a cauliflower and then we could see which of them is
funniest.
I say 'decided', but admitting the possibility is already enough.

Or, if you want to make it even easier: sunsets are moving, if you insist on being a critic in the evening.
But is there something you would rather not suddenly remember, like everyone you know being killed by someone who suddenly appeared, as if out of nowhere, but you weren't killed?
Or everyone you know having everything taken away from them, but you were allowed to keep what you liked and if you saw something better you were allowed to swap.
If you know how to grasp at your heart, you have moments now and then when you can speak to yourself like a critic in the theater who says: don't let me die now when I have to keep calling myself back and reminding myself what has happened because the play doesn't.

In a poem by Cavafy a young man from Sidon says that
Aeschylus gave up something when he didn't have anything
inscribed on his tomb except the field of Marathon being
witness to his bravery, and the long-haired Persian found out
about it too — I first read it as the young man from Sidon
finding that Aeschylus should have continued to speak as in his
plays and not suddenly like someone in a bar telling how he'd
taught a lesson to the man who thought he was small and weak,
but afterwards I see that the young man only says that even on
his last day he should have thought about his plays as well and
not just about that afternoon in the sun, facing the Persians

You give up something
by saying you were brave,
not just that you marched with
an army that took half a day
to pass by.

But it's not the first thing you've given up,
like on a chessboard,
and your opponent
didn't notice until the end of the day
that you'd got more in return.

Contents

- 5   For in the soup or salad, or when you want to decide for others as if you can say, yes, you want to be king of Persia
- 6   The comparative method
- 8   The managers of the world
- 10   Model
- 12   Selling
- 13   Say you're waiting for a victory, somewhere, before you ask the price, and the reply will be, thanks for the news about you, now I am up to date
- 16   The border
- 18   Today's classification problems
- 20   Could you explain again what you are trying to do or want to do, for instance, what can you say about Iraq?
- 23   If you want to wait for an answer anyway, wait for the blue sky to give you one, and remember a poem by Czesław Miłosz
- 24   Deciding what is a public good is also a public good, but every evil dictator can boast about the other public goods he has on offer — please, have another, no need to worry, there are plenty
- 26   Do you feel suddenly pierced by the arrows of time and how long before you will feel it again?
- 28   Nothing, nothing, nothing
- 30   One day
- 32   The abolition of debts
- 34   Not the highest law, but the beginning

36	Like a law or a poem, for the Salafists or Constitutional Originalists, and are we now suddenly allowed to make jokes about what you're afraid of?
38	One is already enough
39	The community gives peace
42	Concerning the limits to freedom of speech, in particular in relation to blasphemy, and the limits to property rights, *with hints how to be a good manservant, by a butler, written down to exercise his handwriting*
47	What can you pay even more tax on and in which ways can you pay tax or what else could you do instead of paying tax?
50	Taxes
53	Lawgiving
56	Making someone king
57	Speech, speech
58	Going back home
59	Into politics
60	The long wave
64	Borrowing from the Greeks
65	Further questions about the relationship between specialization and temporary employment contracts
68	For a day
70	Not really rich
72	You know more about what you have been given than you do about who you are talking to
73	Thank you, and what are you, a historian in a hurry or a hesitant futurist? Or: I will do what you have hastily asked of me, but then I don't need to go to your funeral
74	Honor
76	Representative
77	On the stock exchange
79	If you want to explain something you can start here
80	Ten, ten, ten
81	The Jews
82	That Jewish
83	The Jews
86	Another one to do again, about cultural Zionism
90	Der Judenstaat

- 92   The promise
- 93   The Jews
- 94   Speak up
- 96   A proposal for Happiness Day
- 107 Deciding
- 108 Back in the USSR, for Faiz Ahmed Faiz and Alessandra Palmigiano
- 110 Sigmund Freud visiting Constantine Cavafy, or vice versa, but they had told each other that wouldn't make any difference
- 112 Giving counsel
- 114 The successors' strategies
- 115 The besieger
- 116 Demetrius Poliorcetes
- 118 Speeches
- 119 In a store
- 120 Procession
- 121 Evening
- 122 State and market
- 123 Looking at the market as if looking at the stars and the state as if looking at the moon in autumn
- 124 Judah Halevi
- 126 Today
- 128 In a poem by Cavafy a young man from Sidon says that Aeschylus gave up something when he didn't have anything inscribed on his tomb except the field of Marathon being witness to his bravery, and the long-haired Persian found out about it too — I first read it as the young man from Sidon finding that Aeschylus should have continued to speak as in his plays and not suddenly like someone in a bar telling how he'd taught a lesson to the man who thought he was small and weak, but afterwards I see that the young man only says that even on his last day he should have thought about his plays as well and not just about that afternoon in the sun, facing the Persians

Now that you have read this book, take this moment to think about making a donation to punctum books, an independent non-profit press,

@ https://punctumbooks.com/support/

If you're reading the e-book, you can click on the image below to go directly to our donations site. Any amount, no matter the size, is appreciated and will help us to keep our ship of fools afloat. Contributions from dedicated readers will also help us to keep our commons open and to cultivate new work that can't find a welcoming port elsewhere. Our adventure is not possible without your support.
Vive la open-access.

Fig. 1. Hieronymus Bosch, *Ship of Fools* (1490–1500)

www.ingramcontent.com/pod-product-compliance
Lightning Source LLC
Chambersburg PA
CBHW051131160426
43195CB00014B/2432